The Heartbeat of GOD

"The Fiery Flame of Love"

Charles W. Warner

First Printing:

http://www.theheartbeatofgod.webs.com

-His Heart Scribe- Publications has allowed this work to remain exactly as the author intended, verbatim, without editorial input.

-His Heart Scribe- Publications

http://www.hisheartscribeinspirations.com

ISBN:13—978-1482679694

ISBN:10—1482679698

...Dedication...

This Is Why I Wrote This Book

I am using my time and talents to tell of the Good-News ... the Gospel of Jesus. God inspires me to write, God breathed living fire, His very presence on the words I write. To the glory of God I pray that we may be blessed to know You to love You always and forever Amen.

Occupy until He/Jesus comes ... Occupy does not mean just to stand our ground. It means to go forward and take back what is ours to claim what is ours in Jesus. In Jesus we have all things. Now if we do not have it take it in Jesus name and use it, walk in it ... receive from God what is already yours. Tearing down walls, building up old wells, tearing down old idols and lifting up the name of Jesus!

We need God in America again. We need

God in America like never before! I bow before You Jesus, You and You alone are my strength and my salvation. Lord lead the way and I will follow You for You are my all in all. Feed on the fire of the Holy Ghost. I for one as a 'Watchman on the Wall' cry out ... We need Jesus in this world like never before! Yes it is dark and getting darker but with God I will not fall down and die to this greatest of callings! I stand! I go forth to proclaim the Good-News to heal, to comfort, to proclaim, to love.

-Isaiah 60:1-

Behold the Lord Jesus is alive arise those who are dead, arise those who are asleep; Arise and shine for thy Light has come. Victory in Jesus our Savior forever our Lord in all things. Jesus is most beautiful.

Who hears the call?

Who will follow Jesus in—

The Call ...

The Out Pouring ...

The Overflow...

Living love set this world on fire a wild fire ever growing hotter, higher ... Jesus You're our hearts one desire. We will run with this wild fire setting our world ablaze with living love. I'm addicted to Jesus because

Jesus is most contagious and the Holy Spirit is the Carrier!

Would You Please Agree With Me In Prayer?

It is my prayer that this book will reach souls, will reach hearts. It is my prayer that in these pages we can hear *'The Heartbeat of God.'* To know God as our *'Fiery Flame of Love'* ... love without limits. It's my prayer, it's my heart's cry that the Holy Spirit would use this book to lead hearts to the Holy Bible and lead souls to Jesus. Jesus ... the one and only Savior of souls and Lord of love.

This book is for bookworms like me.

This book is for those who love poetry.

Most of all, this entire book is all about saying—

J♥ E ♥ S ♥ U ♥ S ...

~WHAT A BEAUTIFUL NAME~

No matter how many books you write however many or few remember to start with the Book, the Bible and the Author there of ... ~God~

"HUMBLE YOUR HEARTS AND HEAR, REST YOUR EYES AND SEE, FALL INTO THE ARMS OF LOVE."

...Acknowledgments...

"First and foremost I want to thank the LORD of my life Christ Jesus because without Him I could do nothing. I would also like to thank my Mother in Heaven, family and friends who stuck by me and encouraged me while I took the time and wrote this book."

"It has been truly a labor of love and I feel like this is one of many *"babies"* the LORD has blessed me to create."

"I am looking forward to all He has planned for me in the future."

God Bless You All,

Love In Jesus,

Charles

...Contents...

-Isaiah 61:1-3-

1— "The Spirit of the Lord God is on Me, because He has anointed Me to preach the gospel to the meek. He has sent Me to bind up the broken-hearted, to proclaim liberty to captives, and complete opening to the bound ones;

2— to proclaim the acceptable year of the LORD and the day of vengeance of our God; to comfort all who mourn;

3— to appoint to those who mourn in Zion, to give them beauty instead of ashes, the oil of joy instead of mourning, the mantle of praise instead of the spirit of infirmity, so that one calls them trees of righteousness, the planting of the Lord, in order to beautify Himself."

..1..

~My Beloved~

You are my Savior ... my Lord ... my Love. You are my substance You are my manna. You are my comfort in the wind and cold. You are my joy when I am young and old. You are my strength when I am weak. You are the treasure that I seek. You are my all in all. You are my tent in turbulent times.

You hide me in the cleft of the rock. You are my Rock ... my Rock of Ages. Rock of Ages cleft for me let me hide myself in Thee. I am safe under the shadow of Your wings.

"Come to Me, all you who labor and are heavy laden, and I will give you rest. Take My yoke upon you and learn from Me, for I am gentle and lowly in heart, and you will find rest for your souls. For My yoke is easy and My burden is light."

-Matthew 11:28-

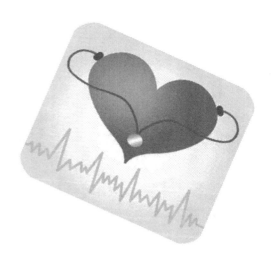

..2..

~A LOVE STORY~

Jesus loves me ... I am His and He is mine .
I am safe in the arms of love ... Jesus
loves His little lamb His beloved ... Jesus
holds His princess . . . He softly and tenderly
whispers, words of love and comfort . . .

"All is well My darling, My dear . . . You are the delight of my soul . . . And I will never let you go. My dove, My love ... I want you to know, I'm always willing to carry you. Wherever we may go."

-Song of Solomon 6:3- "I am my Beloved's, and my Beloved is mine. He is the one who grazes his flock among the lilies."

-Song of Solomon 7:10- "I am my Beloved's, and His desire is toward me."

..3..

~Awake My Bride~

The Bride is awakening behold she is even now opening her eyes to see the all-consuming passion in the eyes of her Bridegroom. There is fire in my Bridegroom's eyes, fire to consume and annihilate all that opposes Him. There is fire in the eyes of my Bridegroom to refine ... to revive this Bride of His. This fire will never die and I cannot take my eyes away from the fiery flame of my Bridegroom.

My Bridegroom is calling. I can hear Jesus my Bridegroom calling me!

Calling me to His side to embrace the One who loves me, the One I love.

Come Away With Me My Love,

Come Away With Me My Dove.

Dear Jesus, take my heart, take my hand, and make me an instrument of Yours. Make my life a beautiful song that glorifies only You.

~My God is an all-consuming fire ... an all-consuming fire that consumes all of me. My God is a Refiner's fire ...

~GOD REFINE ME FOR YOUR GLORY~

..4..

~I Am the Bride of the Lord Most High~

I Am the Bride of the Lord Most High, I am set on fire to dance in the desert place and watch the desert bloom.

-Luke 4:18-19-

I dance and sing the songs of the redeemed.

I pray, I proclaim, I prophesy ... Jesus is most contagious. My feet are Holy every step I take is Holy ground. I pray, I decree my feet to be on fire from on high.

God, set your Bride's feet on fire, set her feet to dancing, dancing with Jesus the Lord of the dance.

Jesus You are the fire in my bones, the flame in my heart, the music that I hear. Release the burning ones those with fire in their bones.

Dance ... Dance ... Dance ...

-Psalm 90:16-17-

My hands are holy.

My feet are on fire.

My heart is His.

I AM MY BELOVED'S AND HE IS MINE!

I will write ...

I will speak ... I will sing...

I will dance ...

We pray, we decree, here and now the passion, the power, the pure love of this dance to go throughout all Israel, all Egypt, all America, all Africa, all the world!

Here and now we prophesy these dead and dry bones shall live; shall live, sing, dance, praise and prophesy before her Messiah; Awake O' Zion; Behold thy King O' Israel. Awake hearts that hunger behold thy light has come.

VICTORY ... SWEET VICTORY IN JESUS.

-Acts 17:28- "Certainly, we live, move, and exist because of Him. As some of your poets have said, 'We are God's children."

-Job 12:10- "In Whose hand *is* the soul of every living thing, and the breath of all mankind."

..5..

~MY EYES~

My eyes go to and fro ... Looking for those who will proclaim My truth ... To know My heart ... Those who will be one with Me in spirit and in truth.

We have the right and responsibility to come boldly before the throne of grace and make our requests known ... We have the right and responsibility to pray to proclaim ...

'This is the day of the Lord.

This is the hour of the Lord.

This is the season of the Lord.

We were born of flesh and bone ...

We were formed of the dust of the earth ...

We are born again of the Holy Spirit ...

We are seated in the heavenlies ...

We are seated in Heaven before God.

As blood bought, Holy Spirit led sons and daughters of God, our spirit is alive in communion with God. We have dominion in Heaven and Earth. Go and be fruitful and multiply take dominion!

~I Am My Beloved's And He Is Mine~

"So shall My Word be that goeth forth out of My mouth: it shall not return unto Me void, but it shall accomplish that which I please, and it shall prosper in the thing whereto I sent it."

-Isaiah 55:11-

"And it shall come to pass afterward, that I will pour out My spirit upon all flesh; and your sons and your daughters shall prophesy, your old men shall dream dreams, your young men shall see visions."

-**Joel 2:28**-

"The Spirit of the Lord God is upon me; because the Lord hath anointed me to preach good tidings unto the meek; He hath sent me to bind up the broken-hearted, to proclaim liberty to the captives, and the opening of the prison to them that are bound."

-**Isaiah 61:1**-

Behold Jesus lives so I shall not make hast or be at want. I shall arise and shine for the Light has come.

"Arise and shine! For your light has come; the glory of the LORD has risen upon you."

-**Isaiah 60:1**-

..6..

~HIS LOVE IS TRUE~

© Rhonda Cox

Times may get tough. The road may seem long. You feel like you are wandering helplessly, not knowing where to turn or what to do. You feel your life is a whirlwind spinning out of control, and your heart just cannot take another blow.

You feel like you are aiming helplessly, feeling lost,

scared, and alone— night comes, and bringing with it the darkness that is unsettling.

The daylight comes, but you do not see the light, you think to yourself, will my day ever be bright. You walk outside, and you can feel the wind. You feel the sunshine upon your skin. You smell the flowers, so beautiful and real. You realize that there is hope that can carry you through.

Deep in your heart, you hear this still small voice. You hear the words of your Savior and Lord. He whispers, "Come to Me My child, let Me carry you, love you, and help you."

He wants to be your helper, to bring happiness and light into your life ... You cry out to Him, "Come Lord Jesus, come, show me Your love, show me Your light." As you run to Him and look upon His face; He wraps you in His arms of love, bringing peace, mercy, and grace.

His love is sure,

His love is pure,

His love never dies,

But lasts forever more.

He is your Light in the darkness ...

He is the Light that never dies.

Cry out to Jesus, and run into His arms.

He promises to never leave or forsake you,

and His love is always true.

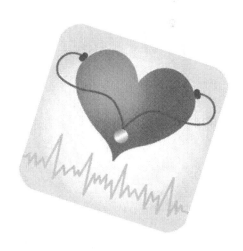

..7..

~THE BIBLE EXPOSED~

People do not reject the Bible because it contradicts itself ... People reject the Bible because it contradicts THEM.

We as Christians must stand up for truth based on the Holy Bible ... Based on the Holy Spirit not on the latest trends.

And, the Word Became Flesh

And Dwelt Among Us.

This is the meaning of life.

Immanuel— God is with us.

-Isaiah 7:14-

Read the "good book" (*the Holy Bible*) it will... Exercise your mind, feed your soul, and bless your heart.

Why Do People Hate The Bible?

—THEY HATE BEING ... EXPOSED!

..8..

~THE HOLY BIBLE~

This is who I Am ...

   The Word of God ...

      This is who I Am ...

God is 'my' Beloved . . .

    and I am 'His' Beloved . . .

Why is it when people go to read the Bible they say, "humm." ... "I've already read this before and I do not need to read this again?" Yet when it is dinnertime we don't say, "What is this?" ... "I don't need to eat again!"

(Feed Your Spirit Not Just Your Face)

"Life without God is like an unsharpened pencil–

... It has no point."

"Relationships give us butterflies—

... God gives us wings."

Be Yourself—

-NOT A CARBON COPY OF SOMEONE ELSE-

You are my Son-shine my only Son-shine You make me happy when skies are gray. You'll never know dear how much I love You please don't take my Son-shine away! Dedicated to the one I/we love ...

~JESUS~

"Lust is not love; love will fill your heart ...

—Lust will drain your soul."

"If we are wise beyond our years, it is because ...

—THE ANCIENT OF DAYS IS OUR BELOVED ONE."

..9..

~THE HOLY BIBLE-2~

The Bible is fresh and new each morning. The Bible is never changing, never out of date, for it is everlasting and true.

The Bible stands the test of time from year to year, age to age, generation to generation.

The Bible will never lose it's power, it's love, it's life,

for the Bible is alive with God's precious personal Words of life. Keep God's precious Words of life ever at hand and always at heart.

~On this road, we call life we must have a road map~ ~ On this road, we call life 'Jesus Take The Wheel' for You are Lord and Savior of our souls.~

It's only by the grace of God in Christ Jesus that anyone can raise their eyes out of the dirt, out of the dust, out of the darkness into God's light.

-John 3:16-21-

16— "For God so loved the world, that He gave His only begotten Son, that whosoever believeth in Him should not perish, but have everlasting life."

17— "For God sent not His Son into the world to condemn the world; but that the world through Him might be saved."

18— "He that believeth on Him is not condemned: but he that believeth not is condemned already, because he hath not believed in the name of the only begotten Son of God."

19— "And this is the condemnation, that light is come into the world, and men loved darkness rather than light, because their deeds were evil."

20— "For every one that doeth evil hateth the light, neither cometh to the light, lest his deeds should be reproved."

21— "But he that doeth truth cometh to the light, that his deeds may be made manifest, that they are wrought in God."

..10..

~THIS BOOK~

This Book (*the Holy Bible*) is the mind of God, the state of man, the way of salvation, the doom of sinners, and the happiness of believers. Its doctrines are holy, its precepts are binding; its histories are true, and its decisions are immutable.

Read it to be wise, believe it to be safe, practice it to be holy. It contains light to direct you, food to support you, and comfort to cheer you. It is the traveler's map, the pilgrim's staff, the pilot's compass, the soldier's sword, and the Christian's character.

Here paradise is restored, heaven opened, and the gates of hell disclosed. Christ is its grand subject, our good its design, and the glory of God its end. It should fill the memory, rule the heart, and guide the feet.

Read It Slowly, Frequently, Prayerfully.

It is a mine of wealth, a paradise of glory, and a river of pleasure. Follow its precepts and it will lead you to Calvary, to the empty tomb, to a resurrected life in Christ; yes, to glory itself, for eternity."

..11..

~THE HOLY BIBLE VS. A BLACKBERRY CELL PHONE~

I wonder what would happen if we treated our Bible like we treat our cell phone.

What if we carried it around in our purses or pockets?

What if we flipped through it several times a day?

What if when we forgot it – would we turn back to go get it?

What if we used it to receive messages from the text?

What if we treated it as if we couldn't live without it?

What if we gave it to kids as gifts?

What if we never traveled without it?

What if we always referred our friends and acquaintances to it?

What if we used it in case of emergency?

This is something to make you go ... "Hmm –Where is my Bible?"

Oh, And One More Thing ... Unlike our cell phone, we do not have to worry about our Bible being disconnected because: 'Jesus already paid the bill.' Makes you stop and think, "Where are my priorities?"

AND NO DROPPED CALLS!

..12..

~The Potter's Hands~

My Lord ... my Maker. You are the Potter and I am but the clay ... I am to be molded and made anew by You today ... Mold me and make me ever new ... form me into what You will for me to be God, have Your perfect will ...

Keep me as Your vessel on Your potting wheel ... Break my will to run ... Form me into the image of Your dear Son.

"SO ARE THERE ANY WHO ASK WHAT THIS IS ALL ABOUT?"

It's about God's transforming power from the inside out.

-Isaiah 64:8-

~On our own we are but dust in the wind yet with God we are clay in the hands of the Master Potter~

~God Fill My Cup And Let It Overflow~

God is not looking for silver vessels or golden vessels He is looking for yielded vessels ... God takes cracked pots and broken cups and He molds and makes us into vessels of honor. God and only God makes monsters into men and men into masterpieces ...

Because He is the Master Potter ♥ God is, good when I am having a bad day ... God takes chaos and confusion and He adds wisdom, truth, and love. Yay for God, His grace, His love ... He is the Potter I am the clay ... I'm willing to be broken to be made anew...

Who Can Relate To This?

-The 23rd Psalm-

The Lord is my Shepherd; I shall not want.

He maketh me to lie down in green pastures:

He leadeth me beside the still waters.

He restoreth my soul:

He leadeth me in the paths of righteousness for His name sake.

Yea, though I walk through the valley of the shadow of death, I will fear no evil: For Thou art with me;

Thy rod and Thy staff, they comfort me.

Thou preparest a table before me in the presence of mine enemies; Thou annointest my head with oil; My cup runneth over. Surely, goodness and mercy shall follow me all the days of my life, and I will dwell in the House of the Lord forever.

..13..

~From Generation to Generation~

.

From generation to generation, we share the greatest of truths, that Jesus is alive. We share the Good News, this Gospel with our children and our children's children. Yes, Jesus is alive; we will celebrate Jesus now and forever more.

I pray— overwhelming, overflowing grace, power, and love ... I pray— the peace of God, the very living, active, personal presence of God, to be with you, to abide with you and your family right now .

GOD IS WITH YOU NOW AND ALWAYS...

—THAT IS WHAT I CALL "GOOD-NEWS."

-Psalm 78:4- "We will not hide them from their children, showing to the generation to come the praises of the LORD, and His strength, and His wonderful works that He hath done."

..14..

~A Testimony I Read On KLOVE.com~

On June 20, 2009, I was involved in a head on collision going at a combined speed of 120 mph with a drunk driver. My neck was broken in three places, C2C5C6, I sustained massive internal bleeding; three broken ribs and both my legs were broken. The EMT pronounced me dead and the

'*Jaws of Life*' cut my broken, lifeless body out of the car.

The ambulance driver raced to the hospital where my parents received notice that their 18-year-old daughter was alive, but barely. I was in ICU for four days with breathing tubes, portal tubes, breathing machines, neck braces, and rods and pins in both legs. It did not look good.

My parents never left my bedside and quoted the Word of God the Living Word over my body and said, "She will LIVE and SERVE the PURPOSES of GOD in HER Generation!" I walked out of the hospital eighteen days later on two broken legs, and was working the drive through at Starbucks serving coffee to the very doctors that helped save my life.

JESUS SAVED ME FROM A BROKEN BODY BUT EVEN WORSE … A LIFE WITHOUT PURPOSE!

He is not finished with me yet and I have a testimony, which is living proof that my work here is not finished! He also saved dad and mom from a broken heart!

DON'T TELL ME THAT JESUS DOESN'T SAVE!

..15..

~THE LITTLE CHILDREN~

D o not resist the children to come unto Me for such is the Kingdom of God.

-Luke 18:9-

We Pray, We Proclaim and We Prophesy—

Come forth, children—

Come forth, pre-teens—

Come forth, teens—

Come forth, youth—

Come forth with songs and psalms.

Come forth with poetry and dance.

Come forth with art and drama.

Come forth with healing in your hands.

Come forth with love in your hearts.

That the children would know Jesus personally.

That the children would know who they are in Jesus.

The children would have dreams and visions, signs and wonders. Their hands are holy; their hands heal the sick and raise the dead. Their hearts overflow with the goodness of God's Shekinah glory.

They Speak Words of Life ...

—The Rhema Word of God

Their feet are on fire, every step they take is holy ground set apart for God and His kingdom alive and active now.

They are wise beyond words in the arts, gifted by God, living on the fire of the Holy Ghost.

They are smart in book knowledge even teaching their teachers, parents, and professors.

They are living witnesses, a testimony to all.

They are fire starters, trailblazers, drawing all to Jesus!

Let us join in with Jesus and our children. Let this be our life, our song, our prayer. I am a promise of God's love, God's covenant revealed.

My Lord God, my passion is to be in Your presence! My passion ... my prize is to gaze into Your eyes! To hear Your heart beat. To fall at Your feet. To rest in Your arms of love.

Dear Jesus, take my heart, take my hand make me an instrument, make my life a beautiful song that glorifies only You.

~I Am My Beloved's And He Is Mine~

..16..

~GENTLENESS IS BEAUTIFUL~

Gentleness is beautiful in the eyes of God above. Gentleness is being kind and showing children love. God makes every child special and unique. Each one of those children need kisses on their cheeks.

Each child is a blessing from our Father up above. Although they all belong to Him, they are here for us to love.

When troubles arise before us, the best thing we can do. Is get down on our knees and God will help us through.

To be understanding parents we must spend time in prayer. That is what God wants from us to show our kids we care.

Each one of our children have so much to give. Though they are young in years, they can teach us how to live.

We thank God for our children no matter what they do. We love and protect them each day through and through.

During those times that we feel weak because things are going wrong. God wants us to lean on Him and He will make us strong.

Children all need gentle hearts to teach them all their days. And parents who will turn to God and follow all His ways.

Each child is so special they are gifts from the Lord. The love they give back to us is our best reward.

All children need gentle hearts to teach them all their days. And parents who will turn to God and follow all His ways.

A gentle touch is beautiful in the eyes of God above. He looks down and smiles when we show children love.

-Psalm 127:3- "Children are an inheritance from the LORD. They are a reward from Him."

-Psalm 127:4- "The children born to a man when he is young are like arrows in the hand of a warrior."

-Psalm 127:5- "Blessed is the man who has filled his quiver with them."

..17..

~YOUR CHOICES~

Every time you make a choice you turn into something a little different than you were before. And taking your life as a whole, with all your innumerable choices, all your life long you are slowly turning either into a heavenly creature or into a hellish creature; either into a creature that is in harmony with God and others, or into someone who is in a state of war with God and others.

To be one kind of creature is joy, peace, and power. To be the other means madness, rage, and eternal loneliness.

'Each of us at each moment in time is progressing to the one state or the other.' —C. S. Lewis

We as Christians in our words and deeds must be led by the Holy Spirit and the Holy Bible. Our words many or few must be truth, wise, and yes sweet.♥

We as Christians must stand up for truth based on the Holy Bible, based on the Holy Spirit not on the latest trends.

Do you want to know true love ... lasting love ... then hold on to Jesus' nail scarred hand.

..18..

~The Road~

At first a man sees sin as a road to adventure ... as a game.

He says, "This is fun ...

I am in control ...

I will live as I please ...

I am the captain of my life ...

I will dance with the devil when I want to ... I can live on both sides of the fence ...

Hey come on I have the best of both worlds!"

Over time the walls start to close in, the floor starts to slope downward.

Sin is not so fun anymore. He starts to see sin is not a party, being a player is not a game it is bondage.
He sees himself not as a rock star but as a prisoner of his own devices.

Sin is an evil, wicked, taskmaster pulling him where he does not want to go, keeping him longer than he wants to stay.

The walls close in, the floor slopes downward.

Sin pulls and tears at his heart, tears at his soul and his body, the more he fights back the tighter the chains become. The more he struggles the more he falls captive to sin. In the daylight he sits in darkness and despair ... hopeless, helpless, lonely, and sad but no way out!

Yet the walls keep closing in, the floor keeps sloping downward.

He cries out, "I fear that this sin that I hold onto ... that holds onto me ... shall drag me lower than the grave."

Sin will take you farther than you want to go, sin will take you to hell.

Sin will keep you longer than you want to stay, sin will keep you forever.

What hope does he have? What hope does any of us have?

This poem is based on **-Romans 7: 14-25-**

KJV **-Proverbs 16:25-** "There is a way that seems right unto a man but the end thereof are the ways of death."

NLT **-Proverbs 11:27-** "If you search for good, you will find favor; but if you search for evil, evil will find you!"

KJV **-Matthew 16:26-** "For what does a man profit, if he shall gain the whole world, and lose his own soul? Or what shall a man give in exchange for his soul?"

-2 Corinthians 5:21- "For Jesus became sin He who

knew no sin that we may become His righteousness love so amazing. Jesus wore a crown of thorns that we may wear a robe of righteousness."

This world is shifting, sinking, sand ... Cry out to Jesus and live ... In a world of shifting, sinking sand Jesus and only Jesus is the Rock of Ages. This world is the Titanic, Jesus is the Ark.

As I travel down this road of life Jesus, take the keys, take the wheel, take my heart. Jesus I am Yours and You are mine.

-I AM MY BELOVED'S AND HE IS MINE-

—Sin will keep you longer than you want to stay, sin will keep you forever.

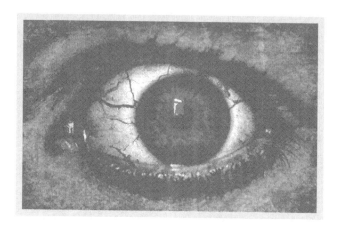

..19..

~Warning~

THE SAFEST PLACE IN THE WORLD OUT-SIDE OF GOD'S WILL IS THE MOST FEAR-FUL DANGEROUS PLACE ON THE EARTH ...

A disbelief in God is not a belief in nothing, it is a be-lief in anything apart from a personal God. An empty heart must be filled. What or who do you seek to fill your heart with? A person who searches for God (*through Jesus)* finds God's heart, God's hand, and God's favor. If you turn away from Jesus and search for evil ... Evil will find you!

-Proverbs 14:12- "There's a way that seems right unto a man but the end there of is death."

-Proverbs 11:27- "If you search for good, you will find favor; but if you search for evil, it will find you!"

Walk with the wise and become wise— Walk with the fools and your life will fall apart.

-KNOWLEDGE WITHOUT WISDOM IS DEADLY-

"The eyes of the Lord are on the righteous. And His ears are open to their cry. The face of the Lord is against those who do evil, to cut off the remembrance of them from the earth."
-Psalms 34:15-16-

~Zombie Nation~

They see but have no sight—

They hear yet never listen—

They take but never truly give—

They walk yet their spirit is dead—

They see the body but not the soul—

They are driven by fleshy hunger and vain lust—

They seek knowledge yet never wisdom —

They want a brain without a heart—

They have no desire for anything past their nose—

CRY OUT TO JESUS AND LIVE—

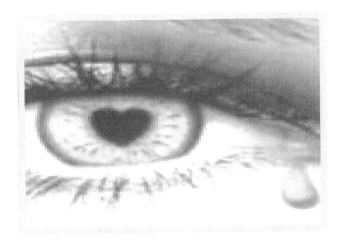

..20..

~BEAUTY FOR ASHES~

G od gives beauty for ashes, strength for fear.
God turns tears of sorrow into tears of
joy. God stores up our tears in bottles, with me
there may be a few bottles. I love to cry because Je-
sus is so sweet; He blesses my heart and I can't help

but cry.   Tears of passion, tears of love, tears that are stored in bottles above. My tears and your tears are stored by God, stored by love, stored in Heaven, in bottles above.

God collects our tears, remembers them, and never forgets. He holds them as a memorial for us. How precious is our God? — Selah

-Psalm 56:8-

..21..

~I AM THE BRIDE OF CHRIST~

I am the Bride of Jesus.

I am my Beloved's and He is mine.

I look to the Rock of my Salvation.

I build my heart, my home on

'The Rock of Ages' all else is shifting, sinking sand.

Dear Lord Jesus, hold my hands in Your precious, beautiful, nail-scarred hands.

Jesus I will follow You ... I will be led by my Lord's nail-scarred hand.

I TRUST, OBEY, AND BUILD —

My life ...

My heart ...

My home ...

On the Word of God.

Not the words of man.

In this dry and weary land of shifting, sinking, sand ...

I BUILD —

My home ...

My heart ...

My life on ...

~THE ROCK OF AGES~

In my life ...

In this land ...

I am led by my Lord's nail-scarred hand.

J♥ E ♥ S ♥ U ♥ S

~WHAT A BEAUTIFUL NAME~

"Except the LORD build the house, they labour in vain that build it: except the LORD keep the city, the watchman waketh but in vain."

-Psalm 127:1-

Build your life ... your house ... and your home on the Rock of Ages (*Jesus*).

Sin is shifting, sinking, sand. If we seek after sin, we end up with a hand full of sand and a heart full of hell! Lay it all down at the feet of Jesus. Jesus alone is worthy to be called Savior.

I don't want to gain the whole world and lose my soul ... I say yes and amen to Jesus my one and only Savior and Lord. Give and take away Lord Your ways are best. Lord that I ... that we ... may know You today, everyday, and forever.

-Matthew 16:26- "For what does a man profit, if he shall gain the whole world, and lose his own soul? Or what shall a man give in exchange for his soul?"

-BUILD ON THE ROCK-

-Matthew 7:24-27- "Whoever hears these sayings of Mine, and does them, I will liken him to a wise man who built his house on the rock: and the rain descended, the floods came, and the winds blew and beat on that house; and it did not fall, for it was founded on the rock. But everyone who hears these sayings of Mine, and does not do them will be like a foolish man who built his house on the sand: and the rain descended, the floods came, and the winds blew and beat on that house, and it fell. And great was its fall."

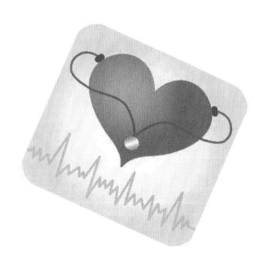

..22..

~A Romantic Poem~

I'm writing you a romantic poem ... a sweet song that will last for all time and eternity. For this is written in the language of love. This is not just a song or a poem this is also a prayer and a promise from the Word of God, from the Spirit of God.

FOR WHAT IS LOVE?

Love is softly whispered across a moon lit pond to the one you love. Love is a dance, a pure, sweet dance of romance. Love lifts up His Beloved in a sweet, heart-felt embrace holding her close to His side. Close yet ever so gentle ... ever so tenderly He holds her hand. Without words, she knows her Beloved is there for her, singing over her, singing to her tender love songs. Dancing heart-to-heart ... hand-in-hand.

She gives him a big bear hug and says, "I am my Be-loved's and He is mine." He says to her, "I love you ... I have always loved you and I always will love you. I am here right now with my adorable, precious, Be-loved I will always be with you ... always and forever ... for we are one."

..23..

~GOD OR GOO?~

How ironic is it that scientist claim they are "intelligent" yet refuse to entertain the idea of *'intelligent design?'*

I'm formed by God and He breathed life into my lungs, into my soul, into my very spirit. I will live forever more for God made me; He knows me and calls me His own.

-Psalm 33:6- "The Lord merely spoke, and the heavens were created. He breathed the Word and all the stars were born."

"The stars shall live for a million years; a million years and a day; but God and I shall live and love when the stars have passed away." —Dr. Henson

God spoke the stars into space in one moment of time, yet with you and I He gave us His heart for all eternity.

Jesus, because of You we can live and love everyday till the stars no longer shine. Till the Rocky Mountains turn to sand. There's one star that will forever shine, that will forever glow oh so bright— the *'Morning Star.'* There's one rock that will stay, that will never go away— the *'Rock of Ages.'*

God created— unless you want to believe in the beginning nothing ... then boom, bang—

BIG BANG EVERYTHING!

Now we are here ... oh no not from nothing, the cosmos started with a dot almost nothing, so everything came from a dot ... a singularity— not from a creative designer?

No thank you! I will trust ... in the beginning, God created. I believe in a living God, I trust Jesus as my Savior and Lord, I am led by a '*Ghost*' the "Holy Ghost," this is not a pipe dream; this is not religion— this is reality.

God holds time and eternity in His hands. How do we explain the movie ET? There may be other life out there– so what. ET does not take away from the Bible, does not take away from the Gospel, the Good News, and does not take away from God's personal promises and living fellowship.

Science points to God not away from God. I talk to the Creator God not just to the created people.

THEREFORE, I ASK YOU—

"In the beginning, '*God or goo*' created you?"

..24..

~COME JUST AS YOU ARE~

Jesus is my Savior, my Lord, my love, my life. Where would I be without Jesus? Where would you be without Jesus? Jesus hears your silent cries. Cry out to Jesus He meets you where you are. Come just as you are all the missing pieces all the wounded hearts.

Come just as you are blinded and beaten, bleeding and scarred. Come just as you are hold on to Jesus, Jesus takes you as you are.

Jesus meets you where you are; lay it all down at the feet of Jesus. Jesus is our *'burden bearer'* He meets us where we are. Jesus gives us beauty for ashes strength for fear, Jesus makes all things new. Jesus saves, delivers, and heals. Jesus paid it all on the *'Old Rugged Cross.'* Now we live we love, we laugh, and we are alive in Jesus.

..25..

~MY—OH—MY THE SONG OF LIFE~

MY—OH—MY what trouble I'm in, my heart be a aching from all this here sin. I got a world of worries that's keeping me down.

MY -OH -MY this heavy burden is too hard to hold. Ain't nobody knows the pain I'm in. Now sin is a struggle, sin is a snare it takes your soul into darkest despair. Now I heard of a story of a man long ago,

He was born to be beaten, born to be bruised. He was nailed to a cross to die for the lost. This man shed His pure blood on the cross only His love held Him there. His life He did give for one reason so that we may live.

Now this man of the cross— this man of Calvary He gave His dear life so that we may be free. Free of the bondage and free of the strife, free to live a brand new life.

Now I call on You Man of the Cross I am so lost. I now take You as my Savior ... my Lord and my Friend. My -oh- My what joy I found in walking and talking each day with my Lord.

Now when this life is over when this life is through when I breathe my last breath, I tell you what I will do, I'm going to look at my Jesus as He looks at me, I'm going to walk with my Jesus, I'm going to talk with my Jesus for all Eternity.

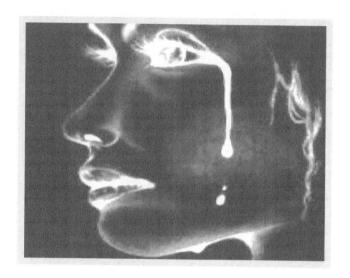

~For Every Girl Who Has Been Hurt~

Girls/Ladies please understand where I'm coming from here. Please read this with an open heart and with open eyes!

~Rules for Guys ... From Girls~

Never say I love you ... if you really don't care.

Never talk about feelings ... if they aren't really there. Never hold my hand ... if you are going to break my heart.

Never look me in the eyes ... if all you do is lie. Does your guy love your skin or love your heart? Meaning does he love only what he can see and feel, or does he love your heart. Does he talk to you heart- to - heart? Does he listen— really listen? Does he really want to touch your heart to be a blessing or are you his slave?

Does he want to use you for what he can get from you? A guy who is always looking at other girls and says, "He only has eyes for you." (*You know if he does*) does not think much of you ... he thinks— "Why buy the cow when he gets the milk for free."

A guy who always calls you sexy, babe, hot ... who sees you as a cuddle buddy does not really love you for who you are spirit, soul, body— it's lust. You will know it's lust not love because he will demand from you or be overly sweet when he wants you but 'ya' know in your heart he is playing you (*and if not you the next girl that would put up with him.*) He should call you beautiful, he should call on Jesus on your behalf. Girls, as the Bible says you should show love to all people but you don't have to be disrespected like that by nobody!

If a guy is playing girls ... If he is playing/lying to girls trying to get her number *"1-815-booty-call-easy,"* then he does not respect girls, does not respect you, does not respect himself. He needs Jesus, don't we all? Now Jesus is the One who knows, respects, loves, listens, and has real dedication...

I'm not part of the sisterhood but I can relate from a guy's point of view. To be honest once again ... Players are like red-eyed rats— they look for easy cheap meat! A guy worth keeping will know where to touch a women— her heart... A real keeper would want Jesus to hold your heart before he ever held your hand.

"A WOMAN'S HEART SHOULD BE SO HIDDEN IN CHRIST THAT A MAN HAS TO SEEK HIM FIRST TO FIND HER."

..27..

~A Moment In Eternity~

May you have many moments of love and joy to share, may your love be strong and grow stronger and sweeter for life— for all time and eternity.

TO WOMEN ...

Don't be a controlling snob. Don't be a money loving, shoe shopping, sister; Don't be in the '*Bad Girls Club*.'
(*Walk in your shoes don't let them walk all over you*).

WHAT I'M SAYING HERE IS ...

Worship God, love your friends and own your belongings; Don't worship your belongings, use your friends, and forget about God.

It's better to live on a hot tin roof than to live with a nagging wife. Let Proverbs 31 be your example. Husbands and wives don't always see eye to eye so in all things look to Jesus.

In marriage build your life, your house, your home on the Rock of Ages not on sinking sand.

Thank God you and your husband are different yet are one in Christ Jesus.

To Men ...

I was told real men don't like to listen to chit chat or details from women? What's that all about? A real man should be loving and good at listening ... Men are (*or should be*) just as romantic and human as women ... Communication is the key to any healthy relationship.

A real man would walk alone through a rose garden stepping on every rose to get to where he is going rather than take the long romantic road with his sweetheart ... Sorry guys, but that's more like a mindless monster than a Christian gentleman! Men should not be labeled as brainless, heartless, monsters ... unless we are one!

Come on men be the head of the house love your wives, let's be men of excellence and integrity let Jesus be our example!

..28..

~IF I HAD A GIRLFRIEND~

Y̊ou heard it said, "If a girl slaps you on one cheek turn your other cheek also." If a girl is cold, give her your coat, (*that way you may win her over as a friend).*

If she is hungry, take her out to Red Lobster or the restaurant of her choice. If she is thirsty, take her to a coffee house for the fancy, flavored coffee of her choice. You have heard it said if your girlfriend asks you to "walk with her a mile, offer to walk with her two." ... You see, your friend may just turn out to be your future loving wife...

If I Had A Girlfriend ...

I would want Jesus to hold her heart before I held her hand. I would want her to be Jesus' Bride before she is my wife. Even if she is never to be my wife may she forever be Jesus' Bride ... His Beloved.

You need a man who sees you are an amazing person from the inside out. A man who sees that you have the most amazing smile. A man that would hold your hand in a slow dance. A man that would let you cry on his shoulder. A man that would listen and love you for you. A man that would be your 'BFF' (*best friend forever*). A man that would love Jesus first there by loving you the best a man can ...

~RELATIONSHIPS~

Relationships are like a mighty wave. We can surf the wave or go down into the deep, blue sea.

Relationships outside of God's will and timing are like drinking sand and calling it fresh water ... So it is in life when Jesus does not have the Lordship of our lives. When we drive without Jesus, we drive into a brick wall every time.

"JESUS TAKE THE WHEEL" © Carrie Underwood

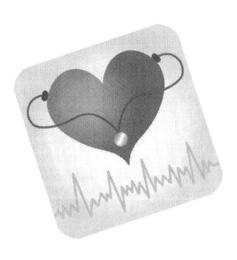

..29..

~WHO HAS LIFTED ME?~

Who has lifted me up? The Lord strong in battle has lifted me up! To war in battle! To roar as a mighty lion? To wear the armor of God! The armor of my salvation! To proclaim salvation is here! Victory in Jesus my Savior forever!

Victory in Jesus is our war cry! Jesus has won and we are one in the Son of God our Savior— Jesus.

Prepare the way...

The time is now...

The place is here...

Rise up...

Take hold...

Go forth mighty man— take the land.

The land is yours claim what is yours.

Take back what is yours.

Run— trail— Blazer.

Holy Fire burn, wild fire blaze across the land.

I am my Beloved's and He is mine!

..30..

~I Am A Soldier~

© Cindye Coates

I am a soldier, a prayer warrior, of the army of my God. **The Lord Jesus Christ** is my *'Commanding Officer.'* **The Holy Bible** is my *'Code of Conduct.'* **Faith**, **Prayer**, and **the Word** are my *"Weapons of Warfare."* I have been taught by the Holy Spirit, trained by experience, tried by adversity, and tested by fire.

I am a volunteer in this army, and I am enlisted for eternity.

I will either retire in this army at the Rapture or die in this army; but I will not get out, sell out, be talked out.

I am faithful, capable, and dependable.

If my God needs me, I am there.

I AM A SOLDIER, A PRAYER WARRIOR.

I am not a baby.

I do not need to be pampered, petted, primed up, pumped up, picked up, or pepped up.

I AM A SOLDIER, A PRAYER WARRIOR.

No one has to call me, remind me, write me, visit me, entice me, or lure me.

I AM A SOLIDER, A PRAYER WARRIOR.

I am not a wimp.

I am in place, saluting my King, obeying His orders, praising His name and building His Kingdom!

I AM A SOLDIER, A PRAYER WARRIOR.

No one has to send me flowers, gifts, food, cards, candy, or give me handouts.

I do not need to be cuddled, cradled, cared for, or catered to.

I am committed.

I cannot have my feelings hurt bad enough to turn me around.

I cannot be discouraged enough to turn me aside. I cannot lose enough to cause me to quit.

I AM A SOLDIER, A PRAYER WARRIOR.

I AM A VOLUNTEER IN THIS ARMY,

AND I AM ENLISTED FOR ETERNITY.

You are my Shield, my Strength, my Portion, Deliverer, My Shelter, Strong Tower, my very present help in time of need

www.whosewill.com

..31..

~I AM IN THE LORD'S ARMY — YES SIR~

The harder we are hit the more we move forward. The battle is the Lord's; we are in the Lord's army. We shout a mighty battle cry, a victory call ——> -VICTORY IN JESUS MY SAVIOR FOREVER!-

This battle is won—

This war is won—

Through the Son!

I arise out of the ashes.

Beauty for ashes, strength for fear.

I stand washed in the Blood of Jesus.

I am forgiven.

I am free.

I am blessed.

I am anointed.

I AM MY BELOVED'S AND HE IS MINE!

I will run, I will run, I will run!

I will fly higher— and higher— and higher still! Jesus makes all things new! I can do all things through Christ Jesus who strengthens me! I will see and I will know Thy Kingdom come to earth as it is in heaven.

I AM IN THE LORD'S ARMY— YES SIR!

..32..

~I Am~

© Deana Hatfield

I am a Warrior of Christ ...   I have all the power and strength I need for battle... I am strong and wise ... I am powerful in my authority ... I am steady and ever watchful ...

I am prepared and cautious ...

I am always at the front line ready to back up my brothers and sisters.

I have armor and a sword ...

I have been called to action ...

I have been given the tools and I have my Captain's favor.

I am a warrior of Christ!

..33..

~THE CHOICE~

May we bow before Jesus now for He is worthy forever. All will bow before the King. We bow before You Jesus as our King ... as our Savior ... as our Lord. Jesus You are our All-in -

All always and forever.

(*The Choice*):

 Jesus is your Savior, Lord and Master by choice or else the devil is your master by default!

"Therefore God has highly exalted Him and bestowed on Him the name that is above every name, so that at the name of Jesus every knee should bow, in heaven and on earth and under the earth, and every tongue confess that Jesus Christ is Lord, to the glory of God the Father."

-Philippians 2:9,11-

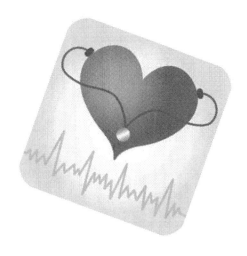

..34..

~THE NEW YEAR~

G od bless you and your family as another year
goes by ... as another page turns in your life
story, as the old clock of time turns we will someday
(*and it won't be long*) gather with our God and with

our family in the greatest family reunion ... the greatest home coming in history ... in His— story!

We shall not count the hands of time or the sands of time for we shall be with our beloved God for eternity. Forever and ever sweeter and sweeter fellowship and love with our beloved God. God, You are our living God for all time and eternity.

With the saints of old and angels all around we even now bow our knees and raise our hands to worship our God, to fellowship with our living God. We are one in the spirit we are one.

WRITTEN FROM THE HEART —

... IN LOVE WITH OUR LORD JESUS.

..35..

~JESUS SHALL BE CALLED~

The Lamb of God ... Savior of man... The Lion of Judah ...The King of kings and Lord of lords...The Light of the World...The Way, The

Truth, and The Life...The Bread of Life...The Living Water... The Wine...

JESUS IS DIVINE ... JESUS IS MINE.

The True Vine... Almighty... Master... Messiah... There is fire in His eyes and healing in His hands.

Creator... Cook... Carpenter... The Doctor... The Door... The Delight of my soul... Alpha and Omega... The Word of God... Son of God... One with God... Teacher... Brother... Redeemer...

FRIEND ... 'BFF' BEST FRIEND FOREVER.

Champion... Hero... Wonderful Counselor... Immanuel... The Rose of Sharon... The Lilly of the Valley... The Rock of Ages... The Bright and Morning Star... The Bridegroom... The Giver of Dreams...

My Beloved— My Love— My Life...

Jesus is a Prophet... A Prince... A King...

JESUS IS MY EVERYTHING!

-IN JESUS I AM-

I am— *"an evangelist"* ... I am— *"a teacher"* ... I am—
"a seer" ... I am— *"a singer"* ... I am— *"a saint"* ... I
am— *"a son of God"* ... I am— *"a poet"* ... I am— *"a
psalmist"* ... I am— *"a preacher"* ... I am— *"a priest"*
... I am— *"a prophet"* ... I am— *"a prince"* ... I am—
*"a promise of God's love— God's covenant re-
vealed."*

..36..

~THE RIVER~

River of Life or River of Death?

Sometimes you think you know the river ... Sometimes you think you know what that old river will bring. Sometimes you think you know what the river is all about.

Then sometimes there is a flood,

Then sometimes there is a drought,

That is when you see you don't know what that old river is all about.

That's when you see you're not in control ...

That's when you see that old river is pulling you down, down, down and surely you will drown.

That's when you look ahead thinking there must be hope.

So you scope what lies at the end of this here river.

In horror, you cry out, "This crooked river will be the end of me for I see at the end of this life's river are the falls and as the river falls so will I!"

As much as I hate to say it, "This here river drops to the land of the living dead, it drops to Hell!"

This wide and crooked river drops to the lake of fire!

How can it be life has no hope, no real meaning?

Life is meaningless— life is hell on earth then hell forever.

This is too much for me to bear why even get out of bed!

I can't go on like this I am lost! That's when with all of my being I cry out, "This is not a river of life it's the river of death!"

I cry, "Is there not a Lord higher than this wretched river?" "Is there not a Lord of truth?" "Is there not a Lord of abundant, lasting life?" "Is there not a Lord over this river of death?" Please oh please if there is such a Lord then I cry out to You, "Lord please be my Lord please save me!"

What is this? How can it be a man who walks on water? This man comes to me and I see a Man with holes in His hands and fire in His eyes. I look into the eyes that hold eternity and I say, "How can this be?" Then He says, "I am Jesus, your Savior and Lord I have come to set you free, come follow Me." He reaches out His holy hand— as I take His hand I see the One who holds eternity is the One who holds me.

This river, this life with all its storms, all its trials can be a river of life when we see that.

-JESUS IS THE LIGHTHOUSE-

Jesus still walks on water and He calls us to walk with Him.

··37··

~WE AS HUMANS~

© Kayla Warner

We as humans are nothing but a vapor that will soon vanish. Sounds depressing, ehh? If I asked you to tell me the definition of 'LIFE' could you do it? Could you explain it? Could you understand it? Hmmm, most of us couldn't.

...But living in a life that is so unpredictable, filled with unexpected surprises, and twist and turns is what makes life so amazing. You never know where your next smile may come from. You never know when the next miracle may happen. You never know when you could have the best day of your life. You never really know what tomorrow has in store for you, much less later tonight. You never know whom you could fall in love with.

...Isn't it an incredible feeling waking up every morning not knowing where God will lead you but you trust Him enough to lead you in the right direction. Life is short ... yeah— yeah, we hear that all the time. But just think of how fast one single day goes by.

...God is coming and you need to live as if He is coming today. STOP putting Him on hold. STOP thinking of the decisions you'll make in the future and make them at this very second. Get far out of your comfort zone and take risks. Make a difference today and don't wait till tomorrow because there is no proof that there will be a tomorrow.

~MY SUMMER VACATION~

© Kayla and Sharon Warner `2004

(MY NIECE WAS 11 WHEN SHE WROTE THIS SHE IS NOW 17)

Most people think of summer as a time that is hot and humid. In my case one summer evening was literally as hot as hell. It was the beginning of summer. It was a time for many changes. I had just finished grade school and I was nervous about what middle school might have in store for me. My two best friends would be attending two different middle schools across town, it seemed our friendships would be lost but not forgotten.

...Two new girls recently moved into my neighborhood. I often saw them walking past my house. Although they were about my age someone would guess they could to be much older. I usually saw them walking the streets, dressed like a Jerry Springer episode, swearing, and puffing on cancer sticks.

...One day my mom said she was going shopping and I had to stay home alone. She said she would be home in one hour. She stated the following rules: no answering the phone, no answering the door and no leaving the house. I said, "okay," and then she left.

...About five minutes later the doorbell rang. I was surprised by who it was. It was the two new girls in the neighborhood. I really wanted to answer the door, but I remembered the rule about not answering the door. Just when I peeked out the window, they saw me and yelled, "Come here!" I thought to myself, 'Why would it be so bad?' They saw me. What was I supposed to do? I went to the door, opened it, and said, "Hi." They looked at each other and smiled. One girl said, "Hi, my name's Jessica and this is my friend, Amy. We were just going for a walk. Want to join us?" Ignoring what my mom said I accepted. (*I thought the girls were cool and if I would hang out with them, we could be friends.*) Jessica said, "Cool, let's go!"

...The girls decided to cut through the park and walk down the railroad tracks. This area was supposed to be off limits. As we were walking, we came to a huge hole in the ground. "Let's check it out," Amy said. It was starting to get dark out and I wanted to go home. I knew my mom would be home in about fifteen minutes. I wanted to impress the girls so I stuck around. We couldn't see the bottom of the hole. Amy kicked a few rocks into the hole. We never heard them hit bottom and it was too dark to see anything down in there.

...There was a very large branch alongside the railroad tracks. The girls told me to pick it up and use it to poke around in the hole to see if I could feel anything. I didn't want to but they began calling me names. I wanted them to stop so I grabbed the branch. I then laid down on my stomach with my face near the hole. Heat was rising from the hole along with a terrible odor.

...I stuck the branch down the hole. The girls began to cheer me on. Suddenly, something or someone grabbed my wrist and began pulling me in. I screamed for the girls to help me, but all I heard was Amy shouting, "Forget you!" Then Jessica said to Amy, "Come on, let's get out of here!" And they left me to be pulled into the darkness. With one final tug on my wrist, I was falling into what seemed to be a tunnel. As I was falling, I could hear screaming that wasn't my own. The odor became stronger, so strong that my eyes began to burn.

...I landed hard on a pile of burning rocks. This shot a pain throughout my whole body. The only light was coming from flames of fire. There were people begging to get out. Their skin was melting off their bodies. Some people had no eyeballs and there were snakes crawling through the openings to what use to be their eyes and crawling out of their noses.

...There were creatures of all sizes that looked like demons. They laughed and celebrated at the torture taking place. I felt nauseous from all the sights. I leaned over and began to throw up. When I looked up the largest of the demons was pointing his long sharp, black, pointed, finger at me! His eyes turned red, and he smiled an evil grin showing all his teeth that looked like a shark's teeth covered in tar.

...He started walking towards me. I closed my eyes. I thought of my family and what I would give to be back in my loving home again. With my eyes shut, I began to pray to God. I was sobbing and crying so hard I felt like I couldn't catch my breath. When I opened my eyes, I found myself lying in my bed on my pillow filled with tears.

I learned a lot that summer night, a lesson for life—

-STAY ON THE RIGHT TRACK, FOR THE WRONG TRACKS WILL ONLY LEAD YOU IN THE WRONG DIRECTION-

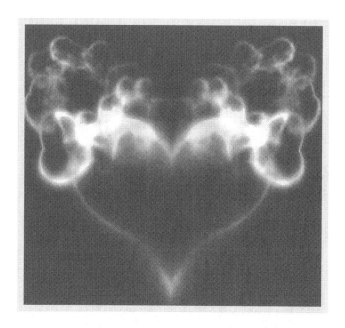

..39..

~MY HEART IS GOD'S HOME~

My God is an all-consuming fire ... all-consuming fire ... consume all of me. My God is a Refiner's fire ... God refine me for Your glory. Dear God, may my heart always be on fire burning hotter and hotter, burning with all the colors of the rainbow, with all the colors of Heaven, with all the colors of Your heart. May my heart be as a raging wildfire wildly in love with my Beloved ... ~God~

May the flames of my heart be as the sweetest of incense because my heart is God's Home -sweet - Home~ My heart sings because Jesus is my Savior. My heart burns because Jesus is my Beloved and I am His. My heart is His home and with Him will I ever abide. Jesus my one and only Love.

Only God can fill an empty heart. Nothing at all can take God's place. And if we try to fill our hearts with anything in God's place it brings heartaches, pain, and loss. Only God is love, life, and joy ever more. In this life there are trials yet God is good, God is in control and God knows best ~ Our Heart ... God's Home~

..40..

~Where The Flower Never Fades~

Where the flower never fades, where the dogwood never dies, where the lilacs last forever ... Where a child never cries, where a lamb lies with a lion cuddling up in perfect peace ...

Where men study war no more, where love abounds, where joy and laughter is all around.

Here there is a King most worthy of His crown. We bow down and sing "Worthy is our King," "Worthy is King Jesus." King of kings and Lord of lords, forever is His reign— Amen.

~You are a Farmer~

As Christians/Jesus followers, we are called to sow seeds of God's Word. His promises and truth, seeds of love and encouragement, seeds of joy and laughter. Planting seeds, and casting seeds into the wind— and the Holy Spirit carries them as He is the wind— planting these seeds in hearts and homes. These seeds grow into mighty trees bearing ***THE FRUIT OF THE HOLY SPIRIT*** for all to share and enjoy. Please share some love today, give some fruit away, knowing all fruit have seeds that will grow .

GOOD FRUIT VS BAD FRUIT

-GALATIANS 5:19-24-

19— "Now, the effects of the corrupt nature are obvious: illicit sex, perversion, promiscuity,

20— idolatry, drug use, hatred, rivalry, jealousy, angry outbursts, selfish ambition, conflict, factions,

21— envy, drunkenness, wild partying, and similar things. I've told you in the past and I'm telling you again that people who do these kinds of things will not inherit the kingdom of God.

22— But the spiritual nature produces love, joy, peace, patience, kindness, goodness, faithfulness,

23— gentleness, and self-control. There are no laws against things like that.

24— Those who belong to Christ Jesus have crucified their corrupt nature along with its passions and desires."

~YOU ARE A FARMER~

You are a farmer because you are always planting seeds. In words, thoughts and deeds we are planting seeds. Seeds of righteousness or seeds of wickedness. The thing about seeds is— Seeds spread and there will always be a harvest. God, we live to glorify You and to bless people. God, as You lead the way we live to plant seeds of love.

- Hebrews 10:24- "We must also consider how to encourage each other to show love and to do good things." "Think of ways to encourage one another to outbursts of love and good deeds."

..41..

~A RAT'S PRAYER~

Dear Lord it is You alone that I desire wash away the mud and mire. Lord take me higher and higher to insure that Your desire would be my desire. To know and love You more each day is what I pray. Jesus I live to glorify you. God hold my paws and make Yourself home in my heart. Dear Lord, may this little rat of Yours be an example of Your love. In Jesus Name – Amen.

~A LAMB'S PRAYER~

If I am a lamb vs. a wolf it's all because I have the Good Shepard. Lord Jesus, Wonderful Savior, You are the song in my heart. Master You cause my legs to leap throughout the valleys ... Jesus You cause me to jump throughout the mountains of spices for You have given me hinds feet on high places.

~A Puppy's Prayer~

I am just a puppy I'm cold and all alone—I can't make it on my own. I am just a puppy won't someone save me from the night? Won't someone hold me tight? I can't help but cry—God save me or I will die! Now who is this Man who shines so bright in the darkest of night? This Man says to me, "I have heard your cry I am here to save you. I am your Savior." As He reaches to me I reach to Him and I find He is good— He is God— He alone is my Savior and Lord. He is my best friend now and forever, He is Jesus.

Won't you trust Jesus today?

~DON'T FOLLOW THE CROWD~

-FOR ME TO LIVE IS CHRIST JESUS-

J— JUST AND TRUE IN ALL HIS WAYS…

E— ETERNAL IN ALL HIS DAYS…

S— SON OF GOD SAVIOR OF MAN…

U— ULTIMATE CHAMPION…

S— SOON COMING KING OF KINGS…

~If you want to know if Jesus loves you —

... look to the Cross~

~If you want to know if Jesus is alive —

... look to the Empty Tomb~

~If you want to know if Jesus is coming back soon —

... look to the Sky~

~If you want to know Jesus —

... look to your heart and invite Him in~

~ROCK OF AGES~

Rock of Ages cleft for me, let me hide myself in Thee. Lord God, over shadow me with Thy wing. Lord, You alone are my soul Provider. Lord, You lift me up higher and higher for You are the wind under my wings.

...GOOD NEWS!

Today someone wrote this to me on You Tube:

> *"Stupid occultist idiot. Nobody cares about your god. Stop advertising jesus."*

I must be doing something right!

JESUS YOU ARE ...

My Savior . . .

My Lord . . .

The Love of my life . . .

Jesus shine all the brighter . . .

Jesus You are the fire in my heart . . .

I will talk —

I will write —

I will sing —

I will dance —

I will celebrate —

I will love Jesus —

..43..

~WATCH THE LAMB~

Lord God, You are my God— my Father —and my Friend. God, You have seen me alone, scared and without hope, yet You loved me so much that You sent Your Son to me! To be my

Shepherd— my Savior— the Lord of my life. Jesus You are the Rock on which I stand all else is sinking sand. Holy Spirit my heart is an open book and You hold the pen.

"When God gives us a word we need to speak, to talk, to share. Other times we simply need to walk away and lay our little heads on our big pillows and let God do what He does best."

BE STILL AND KNOW I AM GOD.

-**Psalm 46:10**- "Be still, and know that I am God; I will be exalted among the nations, I will be exalted in the earth."

Silence is not a sin— Be still and know that God is God. This means turn off your cell phone, turn off your lights and turn on your heart to hearing from God. On the other side of the coin on a busy Monday we can sing and hear from God. Whistle while you work and praise God all day long!

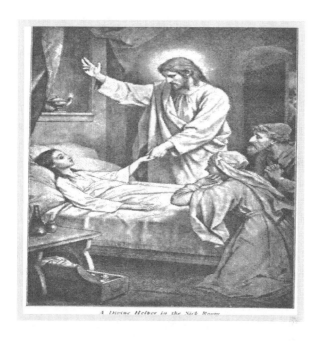

A Divine Helper in the Sick Room

..44..

~THE HEALING HANDS OF JESUS~

© Nina Luolakari

Touch our lives and touch our world. Move within every cell and every soul. Transform us that we might radiate Your wholeness and healing as Your companions in healing the world. Let healing abound— let every act and every word bring joy and wholeness to all creation. In the name of the Healer Jesus, Amen.

A PRAYER FOR YOU AND YOUR FAMILY

Strong, flexible bones, muscles and tendons. Proper alignment, sharp eyes, healthy hearts, powerful lungs. Our blood is strong because Jesus blood is almighty. We proclaim total healing spirit, soul and body in Jesus name.

-Isaiah 61:1-7-

1— "The spirit of the Lord God is upon me. Because He has anointed me *to preach good tidings to the poor*; He has sent me *to heal the broken-hearted, to proclaim liberty to the captives* and the *opening of the prison to those who are bound.*"

2— "He has sent me to *proclaim that the time has come when the LORD will save his people and defeat their enemies*. He has sent me to *comfort all who mourn,*"

3— "To give to those who mourn in Zion *joy and gladness instead of grief, a song of praise instead of sorrow.* They will be like *trees that the LORD Himself has planted. They will all do what is right,* and God will be praised for what He has done."

4— "They will rebuild cities that have long been in ruins."

5— "My people, foreigners will serve you. They will take care of your flocks and farm your land and tend your vineyards."

6— "And you will be known as the priests of the LORD, the servants of our God. You will enjoy the wealth of the nations and be proud that it is yours."

7— "Your shame and disgrace are ended. You will live in your own land, and your wealth will be doubled; Your joy will last forever."

..45..

~LIVE AS IF JESUS IS RETURNING TOMORROW~

L ive as if Jesus is returning tomorrow by believing and receiving Him as Savior and Lord today... In a dry and weary land where there is no water, JESUS is our Living Water. In a land of sinking, shifting, sand JESUS and only JESUS is the Rock Of

Ages.

Jesus may return tomorrow— He may return today. Jesus will part the eastern sky and we will meet Him in the air and so shall we ever be with the Lord. I know when Jesus is returning it will be God's good and perfect time.

Let's live to give— Let's live to love every day. Jesus is with us today in our hearts.

This lifetime is like a vapor, a moment in time, let us store up treasures now that will last for eternity.

People are meandering the world every day, going about their business — hastily wasting their life away on everything else— not creating a time nor place for the King who created them. Time goes by, eternity closes in— have you chosen eternal intimacy or eternal separation of love? Eternity started the day you were born.

..46..

~THEY THAT WAIT UPON THE LORD~

They that wait upon the LORD shall renew their strength; they shall mount up with wings as eagles; they shall run, and not be weary; and they shall walk, and not faint.—

-Isaiah 40:31-

I came through a chicken pen. The chickens are pecking at each other— pecking at the dirt, the dust of the ground— eating bugs... I say, "I belong to Jesus. I am not of this world I am of my Father's Kingdom."

Jesus smiles and I follow Him...

Jesus leads me to a lush, green valley. I declare: "How green is my valley because Jesus is my Shepherd." **-Psalm 23-**

Jesus says, "Come up here." So I say, "I am an eagle ... I spread my wings and He lifts me higher and higher still for He is the wind beneath my wings."

While soaring, the atmosphere becomes charged with the very presence of God. There is lightning and thunder, Holy wild fire fills the air.

I am now a phoenix— a bird of fire. I feed on this fire. (*My God is an all-consuming fire, a Refiner's fire. I feed on fellowship with God*). I hear God saying, "Prophesy my son, my daughter, intercede— proclaim My Word as seed to the Nations."

-Psalm 2:8- "Ask of Me and I will give you the nations for your inheritance, and the ends of the earth for your possession."

I send out seeds to the Nations. The Holy Spirit as a mighty wind carrying the seeds, the seeds are red hot, ablaze in fire. The seeds burst open and now the seeds are too many to count, seeds carried to the Nations— carried to the hearts of humans.

Jesus, You are a seed in our hearts infused with love— a fiery passion, an eternal wild fire, most contagious...

I am addicted to Jesus because Jesus is most contagious and the Holy Spirit is the Carrier!

I want to fly like an eagle to the sea—

I want to fly like an eagle let it be—

I want to fly like an eagle Holy Spirit carry me.

Fly like an eagle because I'm free.

Holy Spirit, You are the wind that lifts these wings.

I fly like an eagle lift me higher and higher still, set me on fire that Your desire be my desire. Holy Ghost, I feed on Your fire for we are one.

..47..

~And The Earth Gave Way~

How do you pick up the broken pieces of life, when such a huge part of you has died? How do you escape the cold iron bars of this cage, when your wings are broken and it's impossible to fly? How do you move on to tomorrow, when time today is standing still?

~My Love~

How do you dress a wound so deep, when all the hope in your little jar has spilled?

When do you start to breathe again? Move again? Live again?

Where do you run to when the storm is so fierce? When your vulnerable, scared, and your child-like heart is pierced?

You run to the one safe place and grasp the hand of your Lord.

You run to the *'Refuge'* ... you run to the *'Rock,'* You run to the *'Rock Of Ages'* and rest under the shadow of His wings.

You cling to the promise of His Word. It is there that you are made whole. It is there your hope is restored. And once again you will find yourself capable of flying.

~Life without love~

Life without love is like a bird without feathers— it's a bird without wings, it's the saddest of things.

Fall into the arms of love and live. Jesus is pure

love .

~SONG~

All I want is to live in Your glory—

All I want is to tell of the story of love ... love that last forever—

All I want is to be in Your presence—

All I want is to be with You forever—

All I want is to sing of this story—

All I want is to live in Your glory forever.

Lord, You are my love ...

Lord, You are my love ...

Lord, You are my love forever ...

~JESUS My love~

I SING LIKE A BIRD ... I SING LIKE A DOVE ... TO THE ONE I LOVE ... TO THE ONE WHO LOVES ME.

IN HIS LOVE—

I WILL WALK...

I WILL SING...

I WILL FLY ALL THE DAYS OF MY LIFE.

..48..

~JOHN 15:5~

I am the Vine, you are the branches. He who abides in Me, and I in him, bears much fruit; for without Me you can do nothing.

Jesus is the Vine— we are the branches. If you stay with Jesus you're a living, active, branch bearing much fruit ... away from Jesus we can do nothing ...

away from Jesus we are a dead twig!

We have a *'Family Tree'* it's called—

~THE CROSS~

WE ARE FAMILY ...

We are Brothers ...

We are Sisters ...

LOOK AT JESUS' HANDS AND FEET ...

These scars are for you ...

This blood is for you ...

WE ARE FAMILY ...

We share the same blood ...

The precious blood of Jesus ...

..49..

~HOME SWEET HOME~

If you hear that I'm dead and gone, that I'm not here anymore— Please don't stay sad and sorrowful. If by chance, you shed a tear or two may those tears of sorrow turn into the sweetest tears of joy knowing I'm not really dead; I'm Home in Heaven singing songs with the redeemed, walking on streets of gold with God.

Pause stranger, when you pass me by—
As you are now, so once was I—
As I am now, so you will be—
So prepare for death and follow me.
To follow you I'm not content—
Until I know which way you went.
Today is the day of Salvation. Take this to heart while you're living because today is the day you have been given. † Only one life to live and it soon will pass ... only what is done for Christ Jesus will last.

~GOD IS LOVE AND LOVE LIVES FOREVER~

They say you can't take it with you ... well you can take love with you. The memories of loved ones knowing we shall meet again in that great forever more. There shall be no more sad goodbyes there because love lives forever and it's love ... it's God Himself who shall wipe away every tear and keep us safe in His arms of love.

Through the years of our lives as time is over taken by eternity remember this—

GOD SO LOVED THE WORLD ...

—GOD SO LOVES YOU AND I.
-JOHN 3:16-

-John 3:16- "God loved the world this way: He gave His only Son so that everyone who believes in Him will not die but will have eternal life."

-John 3:17- "God sent His Son into the world, not to condemn the world, but to save the world."

-John 3:18- "Those who believe in Him won't be condemned. But those who don't believe are already condemned because they don't believe in God's only Son."

..50..

~A TREE IS A FRIEND~

A POEM AND INFORMATION ON TREES—

... AND WHY WE NEED THEM.

A tree is a friend who will stand up tall for you. A tree will never walk out on you. A tree will always show its true colors.

A tree will give you a shady spot on those long, hot, dog days of summer. A tree will protect you, your family, and your home from the mighty winter winds of *old man winter.* What's not to love when trees breathe in pollutants and breathe out pure oxygen. If you give a tree a start, it will find its way into your heart. Trees will grow on you.

PLANT A TREE TODAY—

             ... ENJOY A BETTER WORLD TOMORROW.

⇒   Trees muffle urban noise.

⇒   A mature tree produces as much oxygen in 6 months as 10 people breathe in a year.

⇒   To produce its food, trees absorb and lock away carbon dioxide, a global warming suspect.

⇒   Trees help clean the air, intercepting air borne particles and absorbing such pollutants as carbon monoxide, sulfur dioxide, and nitrogen dioxide.

⇒   Trees shade and cool the air and surface. Shade can cut heat some 20 degrees, chopping down energy cost.

⇒   During cold seasons, trees act as windbreaks and save on heating. Trees save you money on heating and cooling— now that's a true friend or should I say— '*tree friend.*'

⇒   Trees fight soil erosion, conserve rainwater, and reduce water runoff and sediment deposits after storms.

⇒   Real estate values increase when trees beautify a property or neighborhood.

TREES ARE MAJESTIC AND MIGHTY...

              TREES ARE BEAUTIFUL...

     TREES ARE A WONDERFUL GIFT FROM GOD...

We have a *'Family Tree'* it's called—

~THE CROSS~

WE ARE FAMILY ...

We are Brothers ...

We are Sisters ...

LOOK AT JESUS' HANDS AND FEET ...

These scars are for you ...

This blood is for you ...

WE ARE FAMILY ...

We share the same blood ...

The precious blood of Jesus ...

..51..

~Jesus My Freedom~

JESUS · · ·

You are my freedom—

My passion —   My prize —

JESUS YOU ARE MY LORD —

My life —   My love —

JESUS YOU ARE MY ONE DESIRE —

Jesus You are the fire that burns in my heart.
My heart sings because Jesus is my Savior.

My heart burns because —

Jesus is my Beloved and I am His.

My heart is His home

and with Him will I ever abide.

JESUS MY ONE AND ONLY LOVE ...

Never water down the Gospel to appease people, The Good News is meant to bring conviction unto repentance. Lukewarm is pacified religion!

"Lets be all the more on fire with a living relationship with God!"

"God cannot give us a happiness and peace apart from Himself, because it is not there. There is no such thing. " —C. S. Lewis"

..52..

~COME BURN IN ME~

ARISE MY BRIDE . . .   ARISE MY LOVE . . .

—THE GRAVE NO LONGER HAS A HOLD ON YOU—

I have a hold on you—

I Am has a hold on you—

I AM THE RESURRECTION AND THE LIFE.

I am yours and you are Mine!

"I am the resurrection and the life. He who believes in Me, though he may die, he shall live. And whoever lives and believes in Me shall never die."

-John 11: 25-26-

DO YOU BELIEVE THIS?

Lord Jesus, I trust in You, I trust that You are the resurrection and the life. Jesus You are my resurrection and my life.

LET HIM WHO HAS EYES— LET HIM SEE.

New Sight—

New Vision—

LET HIM WHO HAS EARS— LET HIM HEAR.

New Voice—

New Song—

LISTEN TO THE SPIRIT'S CALL—

Calling you by name— Calling you by heart. Deep
calling unto deep—

In this dry and weary land where there's no water.
Lord You are my *Water*— You are my *Living Water*—
You are my *Bread of life.*

THANK GOD FOR HIS SON—

A GIFT TOO WONDERFUL FOR WORDS ...

-2 Corinthians 9:15-

~OUT GROW~ I see a mighty wave racing across
the land. I see a mighty title wave of the blood of
the Lamb of God crashing into the church breaking
out of the four walls of the church.

~OUT GROW ... OVER FLOW~ Open the flood gates
of heaven let it rain ... More and more let it pour
wind ... rain ... and fire! Let it flood with the blood
of Jesus!

—The work of the Gospel— the Good News is not to
close with a lesser display of the Holy Spirit's power
than that which marked it's beginning...

~PRAY ... PROPHESY ... PROCLAIM~

With my friends I want to start singing, Bible reading, poetry and art-work at the parks. (*This would be an exciting living witness*) yes just

like the early church and like the 70's Jesus people...
The Holy Ghost hippies and hillbillies. Who's with
me? :)

Honestly, we should not just use our gifts and tal-
ents in the church building on Sunday morning
locked up behind four walls. Was it not Jesus who
said— "Go out into all the world?"

-Matthew 28:18-20-

PRAY ... PROPHESY ... PROCLAIM—

Jesus is Savior over this city, Jesus is Lord over this
land. This park is a habitation, a home-sweet-home
for the Holy Spirit. Create an atmosphere here, an
atmosphere of hunger for more than average ... for
average is the enemy.

We cry out for more than the average mundane,
there must be more than just living and dying. Cre-
ate in me a clean heart, a heart that cries out to God,
a living God, for only God can satisfy a hungry heart.

I'M HUNGRY FOR GOD ...

My heart travails—

My soul shakes—

My body aches—

ONLY GOD CAN SATISFY MY HUNGRY HEART.

We will sing in the parks. Sing hymns, 'I love to tell the story of Jesus and His love.' We will sing songs of yesterday and songs of today.

We will lift up a joyful noise, the Lord has made me glad, the joy of the Lord is my strength.

-Psalm 150-

We will sing a new song, we will sing in the glory by the glory of God. Songs that reach a new wave length. We will sing that we all may be one worshiping at Jesus' feet.

We will sing praise and worship songs to go forth to be heard, to draw all people, to fall face down at the foot of the Cross that the lost will be found in Jesus.

Glory, grace, power, and love without limits because God has no limits.

May the very air radiate His presence, may the atmosphere be charged with Holy Ghost electric wild fire, may there be a heavy, heavenly incense in the air.

May the earth tremble praising Your Holy name.

Angels in the atmosphere Lord God open and close doors. God open old wells and open new portals.

With God it's our mission ... our calling to glow to show forth God's glory and live out His love. Planting prayer and the Gospel in hearts and in the land.

Dear God,

Infuse me with Your glory ...

Capture me with Your love ...

Surround me O' Lord with Your presence ...

My God is an all-consuming fire— an all-consuming fire— consume all of me. My God is a Refiner's fire— God refine me for Your glory.

Dear Jesus,

Take my heart, take my hands, make me an instrument for Your glory, make my life a beautiful song that glorifies only You ...

Dear God,

Infuse us with a love for Jesus that is most contagious. I'm addicted to Jesus because Jesus is most contagious and the Holy Spirit is the Carrier ...

..54..
~LET IT RAIN~

As deep speaks unto deep, as iron sharpens iron. ~IMPARTATION~ ... May my gifts, talents, and love be shared with your gifts, talents, and love because we are family and friends.

BY THE VERY BLOOD OF JESUS WE ARE RELATED.

May we know God and share God's love.

~IMPARTATION~

In the courts of Heaven in the Throne Room of God stands a green eyed young lady with red hair, pig tails, and freckles. This girl is speaking with fiery passion praying to Jesus—

THIS IS HER PRAYER—

Jesus, I want my sister to have all my gifts and my talents to share ... all the love I would have shared ... the wisdom I would have imparted.

Jesus, give these to my sister and give much more than I would have had if I was not aborted.

Please Lord Jesus, let my parents know how much I love them and how much You love them; impart to my parents my talents, my gifts— Lord send my passion and my love for my family to share ...

Jesus I pray, send Your love, Your passion for my family to share, for the whole wide world to share. All the Saints of old, Abraham, Isaac, Jacob, Peter, Paul and Mary. Moses, Martha, and Smith Wigglesworth join in one accord saying— "Yes I agree with this prayer Lord, we pray as one— Send our passion, our faith, our love, send our gifts, and our talents. Send the anointing we had while we had our time on earth. Jesus rain down Your glory, Your grace, Your love, Your blood covenant, rain down Your presence on all the people."

Dear Jesus, hear our call. We call on the former rain. Rain down all the mantles we have worn, all the seeds we have sown, rain down on this generation.

Jesus says, "Amen granted!" (*slamming down His Judge's gavel hammer*) "I see my beloved bride crying drip, drip, drip, tears of passion, zeal and love. Beloved you are My inheritance and I am your Inheritance. As deep calls out to deep, as iron sharpens iron ... ~*IMPARTATION*~

My love is ever poured out to you, My heart is yours and your heart is Mine, we are one. I impart the full impartation on you now. Former rain— let it fall, Latter rain— let it fall in full. Feed on the fire of Holy Spirit."

(*Seed time and harvest as one*) any of us can now pick up any mantle through ... ~*IMPARTATION*~

LATTER RAIN is— Points of God's glorious light illuminating countless truths, all truth in scripture, in the fullness of revelation.

LATTER RAIN is— A flood of the blood of Jesus. Jesus being lifting high above all and the man made Jesus crumbling to dust.

"Things which eyes have not seen and ears have not heard, and have not entered into the heart of man, ALL that God has prepared for those who love Him. For to us God revealed through the Spirit."

'The work of the Gospel, the Good News is not to close with a lesser display of the Holy Spirit's power than that which marked it's beginning.'

...About the Author...

"I am using my time and talents to tell of the Good-News ... the Gospel of Jesus. God inspires me to write, God breathed living fire, His very presence on the words I write. To the glory of God I pray that we may be blessed to know Him and love Him always and forever, Amen."

Charles Warner is a *'poet after God's own heart.'* He has written this collection of poems with the desire for them to draw the readers into a deeper more intimate relationship with Jesus! Charles resides in Rockford, Illinois with his family and friends. He spends his days seeking to know God in an even deeper way. This collection of poetry is just one volume of many that he has already written and is awaiting the publishing of the complete 2-book set, "The Heartbeat of God!" "I for one as a 'Watchman on the Wall' cry out ... We need Jesus in this world like never before yes it's dark and getting darker but with God I will not fall down and die to this greatest of callings! I stand! I go forth to proclaim the Good-News to heal, to comfort, to testify, to love!"

-His Heart Scribe– Inspirations Devotional Magazine is blessed to introduce you to one of God's most devoted scribes.

There are those people that come along and say, "I know the LORD." Then there are those that come along and "truly" do.

This man is a 'rare jewel' and possesses the divine gift to write what God's heart whispers. Very few are able to express the deep and hidden things of the Father's heart with the honest and pure passion that Charles portrays.

This month we are honored to have him visit with us and share some of his amazing talents for writing. Please take a moment and allow us to introduce to you this extraordinary poet.

Hhsi: Hello Charles and welcome. It's a blessing to have you with us this month!

Cww: Thank you, and I'm glad to be here. I am truly blessed to be a part of -His Heart Scribe- Inspirations Devotional Magazine.

Hhsi: First of all, let me ask you what drew you to the LORD'S ministry of the "scribe?"   In other words ... what was the birthing process of your gift of writing?

Cww: God drew me to writing poetry when I was a teenager. I did not want to write, I thought and said to God— (*"poetry is just for little girls"*). Well let me say I am blessed to know God is persistent. God kept speaking to me, whispering to my heart to write ... saying, "He would always be with me to anoint my heart, my hands and my pen." God knows me better than I know myself, truth be told I don't know who I am without first knowing who He is. In other words in seeking God's heart I find my own heart beats with His. When I am lost in love then am I found in God.

Hhsi: When you think back over the years you have written poetry, messages and prophetic words which area do you feel you excel in more so than the others?

Cww: Well I started writing poetry, then later God would have me keep a notebook beside my bed so I could write down my dreams. Later God let me know that I am a seer so I started recording, writing down my visions. Now God is speaking to me prophetic words, poetic words, words of wisdom and love first thing in the morning or late at night or while eating tacos at Taco Bell lol. In other words, God speaks to me anytime He wants to. God, more love, more power, more wisdom. God I am crying out for more of You for only You will do because You alone are my God ... my Daddy— my All-in-All, Amen.

Hhsi: You shared a poem you had written for your mother a few weeks ago, was she a great influence that drew you into a closer walk with the Lord?

Cww: My Mom was a great influence in my walk with Jesus. My Mom would play the old *'8-track tapes'* and the *'vinyl records'* in the living room playing the 'Old Time Gospel' —'Southern Gospel' like— *"Will the circle be unbroken, The Old Rugged Cross, On the wings of a snow white Dove."* I did not like hearing those songs at first, but honestly those songs spoke to my hungry heart and only Jesus can satisfy a hungry heart. Now days I think of my Mom walking with Saints, talking with Angels, and dancing with Jesus on streets of pure gold. I to shall sing, dance, and glorify God forever in that great forever more. Eternal life starts the day you invite Jesus in your heart. Jesus The WAY, The TRUTH, The LIFE.

Hhsi: You have blessed so many of God's people with your wonderful and thoughtful writings, how does being one of the Lord's great encouragers influence your day-to-day life outside of your writing?

Cww: Well, for example— I write the written Word and speak the spoken Word. Let me share a story! I was walking in Wal-Mart and I could feel electric waves flowing though me I thought, "Is there a live wire here in this building?" Then suddenly I knew, "I am the live wire and the Holy Ghost is the fire I feed on!"

At Wal-Mart I was walking down the toy aisle and God spoke to me to pray, to prophesy over the Barbie dolls and Teddy bears that God's anointing, that God's Holy Presence would abide with the Teddy bears and Barbie dolls, that the Holy Spirit Himself would go where the toys go to heal broken bodies, to minister to souls, to draw hearts home to Jesus. When you glorify God then you can bless people.

Hhsi: We have also been blessed with the honor of introducing your new book "The Heartbeat of God" in our –Aspiring Authors Showcase this month could you share with our readers what inspired you to write this book?

Cww: After collecting so many poems God was like, "Charles are you going to keep your poetry in cold storage or are you going to share your gifting, your talents with the world?" So I started looking into how I could share my poetry to shout 'Jesus is alive on the highest mountain, to cry out Jesus lives in the lowest valley.' I met Cecile Jo just before Christmas of 2012 and from there on Cecile has encouraged and helped me to collect my writings to share in my first book called— *"The Heartbeat of God."* I know there are a billion books out there but this one is my baby. God called me to write this one.

Hhsi: If anyone wanted to get a book published what is the most important goal that they would have to meet in order to do this in their own lives?

Cww: I would say, know God's heart and know He is wisdom, knowledge, and art. God is worthy and the Giver of all good gifts. God is the Author of life, seek God's heart. You want living words worth reading. We don't need more books in this world just to say I wrote my own book. We do need living words to set our hearts on fire, a passion and a desire to know God heart-to-heart. No matter how many books you write however many or few, remember to start with The Book, The Bible and The Author there of — ~God~

Hhsi: What's on your plate next in the publishing and writing area?

Cww: My next book will be a collection of my favorite hymns. Hymns are songs, prayers and poetry set to music. I want all generations to remember the great old hymns and to learn the hymns for the first time. So I will be sharing hymns as poetry because so many of the hymns started out as poetry. I will also be sharing more of my poetry, prayers and prophetic writings.

Hhsi: If anyone would like to get in touch with you, how could they do this? Do you have a website or an email they could contact you on?

Charles W. Warner
My website and website email is —
http://www.theheartbeatofgod.webs.com
charleswarnerbooks@gmail.com

 My Facebook is —https://www.facebook.com/charles.w.warner

My email is—
catfishboy123@yahoo.com
musclemanchaz111@aol.com

Hhsi: Charles, it has been such a blessing getting to know you and your work for the Lord. Is there anything else that you would like to share with our readers?

Cww: I would like to say it is my honor and a great blessing to be in this magazine to share the Gospel, the Good-News, to love and be loved. If Jesus is your Beloved Lord and Savior then we are blood Brothers and Sisters —Family by blood— by the very blood of the Lamb of God. It's good to know in Jesus we live, move and have our being. Some day, and it won't be long we shall have the greatest Home Coming Family Reunion ever. To dance on the streets that are golden. We will dance on the streets that are golden the glorious Bride and the Great Son of Man .

"Humble your heart and hear, rest your eyes and see, fall into the arms of love and live."

J♥E♥S♥U♥S

Hhsi: It's been an honor introducing God's work through you to everyone. We pray that you will continue to be filled and led by His precious Holy Spirit in all that you do. May this year 2013 be your greatest and most blessed thus far! Thank you so much for sharing with us.

Look for our cover with author Charles W. Warner here: **http://www.magcloud.com/user/cjoh**

Be sure to get your **"free"** PDF download!

ALSO In This Issue ....

Powerful, testimonies of God's grace and mercy in the lives of His people. Devotionals that truly will bless you and encourage you to keep on pushing through whatever you may be facing. Poetry that truly expresses the love for and from the Father to each one of us His children. Powerful teachings, preaching and messages for a deeper, closer walk with the LORD. An intimate look into the lives of those living with disabilities and in spite of their limitations continuing on with a life devoted to serving. Authors that have given of their time to write the ~heart whispers~ from the LORD. An up close look into the lives of those in service in the Kingdom.

AND MUCH MORE! So sign up NOW with your email address at:

hisheartscribepublications@gmail.com

"Who knows— You the reader might just be our next aspiring author and our cover feature!"

...Notes...

...Notes...

...Notes...

...Notes...

May this book point to The Book The Holy Bible. May this book point To the Rock of Ages (Jesus)

God Bless you and yours

celebrating Jesus

60 yrs

Loving people

To Apostle Don and Donny Lyon

from Charles Warner

Made in the USA
Charleston, SC
09 May 2013